OUT OF THE BLUE

OUT
OF THE BLUE

Poems by

Fran Carbonaro

fmsbw
San Francisco, California

ISBN: 979-8-9894133-5-5

"Psyche's Other Box" was first published in *Reverberations III* as a response to Monika Rosa's painting "Collective" (Sebastopol, CA: RiskPress Foundation, 2023).

"A Shakespearean Apology" was first published in The Redwood Poetry Anthology (Arcata, CA: Redwood Writers Center, 2023).

Cover Art by José Ramón Lerma

Author Photo by Kathleen MacGregor

fmsbw

San Francisco, California

For Alan & Ted

"Gather your emptiness where you can and begin again"

—Jack Crimmins

FOREWORD

It seems appropriate to begin an exploration of Fran Carbonaro's first full-length collection of poems with a quote popularized by John Lennon: "life is what happens to you when you're busy making other plans." The title *Out of the Blue* suggests the surprising, improbable, unintended, and disarming nature of much of what human beings encounter as they move through their days on earth. It also intimates the shift from sadness (the blues) to some other emotional state.

The poet toggles between tumult, division, and epiphanic resolution. There is a strong spiritual presence, though the source is more secular, human or feline than divine. Carbonaro is a confessional poet whose dialogue is often conducted with someone whose presence has redirected her thoughts and actions – a parent, a childhood acquaintance, or someone who has caused her harm. Sometimes these are the same person.

Countercultural movements from civil rights, women's liberation, and anti-war protest of the 1960s remain a strong thread in the poet's imagination, political activism, and life experience. The poem "Witness" dedicated to Carbonaro's mother. It opens with the lines:

> *Something led me right to the rack*
> *Was it you, Mom, who nudged me*
> *there where they were squeezed in*
> *between several war-torn arrivals?*

The reader's mind may connect "the rack" with a mode of torture. The reference to "war-torn arrivals" conjures what? Returning soldiers, undocumented immigrants, exiles? Traveling deeper into the poem, we discover that this is a clothing rack in a thrift store, housing a pair of hot pink designer slacks "too small and in need of alteration" that the poet imagines wearing them in the future that has become today. Along the way, the story of her mother's oppression beneath the battering presence of the father and the daughter's struggle to free if not her mother, then herself from this metaphorical rack of this legacy through a series of avenues.

> *Good, good, good, I even went to church for a good while*
> *but could not confess that I dreamt of pushing him off the roof.*
> *I left the church, surfed the 60's, no idea what I wanted to be*

The poem ends with the image of the poet "kneeling" on the salve of self-preservation wearing the bright pink pants chosen for her by her mother and surrounded by "blues of endless sky / the black of damp, rich earth."

Interesting for a poet who has devoted her life to music – as jazz singer, songwriter, theater performer, and vocal coach – her poetic meter is more incantatory than strictly melodic. As in classical drama, one can hear the echo of the poet in soliloquy upon a stage conjuring characters and moments in history to honor, to explain, to mourn, and ultimately to heal.

Carbonaro devoted herself to the care of a now late husband, who she met unexpectedly later in life. The pain of this loss, compounded by early family trauma, run rapids through the river of her verse. The poet herself appears in nearly every poem as a stone over which these counterflowing currents swirl, sometimes threatening to pull her down. From "Bear":

> *In the crumbling barn of my mind*
> *chaos chases me from room to room*
> *My beloved dies before my eyes*
> *I cannot save him. I am suffocating*

In poems that surround this one in the collection, the poet works to lean on love as a force more powerful than all that curveballs like cancer and dementia threaten to strip away and override. She fights in "Crash Course" to say "YES" to the beauty that lies within even the most crushing of truths.

This dramatic polarity of forces also appears in the form of societal injustice. In "Suburban Wall", a poem whose title refers to a 1972 documentary exposing redlining and other forms of racial segregation in various communities, including San Leandro, whose population was 99% percent white, despite being adjacent to predominantly black Oakland.

Playing our roles
losing each other
traveling in opposite directions

In the poems that comprise *Out of the Blue* we swing between having a clear sense of the scene before us and the presentation of a situation in which the key elements are left ambiguous. The power of the collection seems somehow to rest on this. In some situations, we can know what lies before us or what has been, and we can wrap our heads around both outcomes and roads not taken. At other times, we struggle to find our bearings and realize that we stand at the center of a profoundly human experience without any clarity about some of the most critical moments and questions of our life or humanity. Perhaps the best we can do is bear witness and echo the *yes* of a kindred spirit.

Tamsin Spencer Smith
San Francisco, CA

CONTENTS

SOUTH OZONE PARK, 1962

Mom's stepmom, my almost grandma
sits in her garden, BB gun across her lap

She sees my eyes grow wide "It's for the
squirrels, they steal my walnuts" she smiles

I feel a chill in the humid heat. This must be
the last walnut tree in South Ozone Park

A borough of Queens, soon on its way to ghetto
today "Save the Squirrels" like a banner, waves

When she goes inside to pee, my 11-year-old self
chases a squirrel away "Don't come back!" I plead

It does and grandma nails it, has to shoot it twice
to finish it off. She owns this corner of the world

I was sent here by my parents for the summer. Why,
I wonder. Here they speak Italian behind my back

Later, she insists on buying me my first bra. I imagine
stuffing the small cups with walnuts, tying the straps

I will fling this gift over my shoulder, run to the
nearest park, feed the squirrels, make new friends

CAROUSEL BALLROOM

One ear pressed against the inside of mother's uterus,
my very own pregaphone taking in the world I'm about
to enter. That last trimester, breathing underwater, in the
warm safety of the womb, listening to the bombs dropping

Leaving her turbulent waters, sensing her apprehension
slipping into our isolated war zone, where delicious food &
loud laugher intersperses with curse words and cries of pain
dotting clutches of fear with feigned joy and savory pleasure

Don't stop moving says my small body: run, play, dance, sing
when the sun shines! Crouch, freeze, hold your breath at night
Years later the loud frenzy of the Fillmore West holds me tight
as my limbs kick fiercely at the darkness 'til it bleeds daylight

Another decade later, I digest the news
You tried to end it twice
first me, then you
abandoning both
stunned silence, long exhale
feeling you and grateful for a heartbeat

SUBURBAN WALL

I searched for the photo for several months
the one of you and me in front of our big house
on a busy street in a small white city next to Oakland

I had been confirmed at St. Leander's only hours before
a big dose of holy moving through my ten-year old veins.
How could I know it would be the only time in this life

I would wear a white veil with a white dress
most of my family gathered round in pride
You dressed in black and parked behind us

Your shiny black Chevy coupe
cherry red Tijuana tucked and rolled interior
Dixie Peach straight up crew

Hands stuffed in pockets
wearing that *give me a break* expression
and ready to roll.

Two ends of the same sorry spectrum
Me in lost innocence
You in dark denial

Playing our roles
losing each other
traveling in opposite directions.

If I could have stepped past my borders
To turn laughing to you
Hey, little Sicily, you don't scare me

THE GIFT

you were sitting there
not rocking, in that chair
by the window
i wanted to say goodbye
it was time to go
my womanhood just
beginning to lift off
smoke curling from
a cigarette dangling
between bent fingers
i wanted to say goodbye
to that heavy thing
you carried on your chest
the air was close
it was time to go
i found your side
a slow lean to kiss
your cheek, leaning
into the barbed wire
to leave the gift
of lips between
your cheekbone
and clenched jaw
i'll see you in a
few weeks
and waited for you
to lift your face
your eyes met mine
and the words
kiss of death fell
from your mouth
they sounded soft
almost tender
frozen in time, light
slanting in long strips
thru venetian blinds

just the two of us
a dark line
a thin wire
a tightrope
between us

WITNESS

for my mother, Rose Ida Pellegrino

Something led me right to the rack
Was it you, Mom, who nudged me
there where they were squeezed in
between several war-torn arrivals?

They were like new and incredibly pink
the perfect match for an exotic tunic I'd found
only days earlier, in another consignment shop
A mission we shared.

You whispered: *these are the real deal*
Salvatore Ferragamo designer slacks
in search of a stick figure and wedge heels
I had to buy them.

Though too small and in need of alteration
I could see them on me with the silvery
Close-cut hair that would someday replace
My dyed and flowing brown mane.

You always liked my hair short like yours
later in life, saying it was so much easier
that way but not saying it was so much harder
for him to grab hold of and drag you around by.

Remember how I sheared mine when you were
diagnosed and how you let yours grow long
when perms wouldn't hold after the chemo
I'd never seen your hair so long and thick.

Cancer got him first and the way was clear
for that brief time to hang loose, to live,
then die in your own particular way
with no one to cook for or answer to.
For years you spread the table with sumptuous

Sicilian dinners, cooked after working all day
in a paper bag factory and years later at Macy's
When the fashion bug bit you.

You'd bring home clothes bought on discount
for the body you wish you had
for your slender daughter who didn't fully
understand all your sacrifices at the time

Back then I begged you to leave him
Find an apartment for just us two
to watch movies, eat tomato soup and grilled cheese
You'd shake your head and say, *he'll just come after me.*

How many years earlier had you gone to your father
asking for help, only to be told: *You made your bed*
Now lie in it. You became pregnant, bore a sick child
then pregnant again, which you tried to end, but failed.

Caught like a mouse in a trap, reconciled to its fate
I watched you drag yourself to work after he'd keep you
awake most of the night: your coffee was strong, like your will
Like a bull, you lowered your head. Suicide was not an option.

You were mother, you were sister, you were friend
I was your confidante and the only other woman in the house
I didn't know how to stop the battering of your body, your soul
Just tried to be all that you wished your life had been.

Good student, good daughter, good friend, good girl
Good, good, good, I even went to church for a good while
but could not confess that I dreamt of pushing him off the roof.
I left the church, surfed the 60's, no idea what I wanted to be,
though by then I knew what I didn't want to be was you

Why was I born, a woman, into this family?

Come look at your late bloomer
My clothes rack is a wild garden
The pastels of renewed innocence
Rose reds of fiery passion, blues of endless sky
the black of damp, rich earth. And today
I wear the bright pink pants you chose
I kneel on the bottom line. Cracked (*Protect and cherish
all life)* and uneven (*especially your own precious existence)*

PATRIARCH

In the name of our father
You proclaim the dark secrets
Of pride and possession

Hoist your weight
Like a vengeful pirate
Protect all the wrong things

Blame those
Who merely thirst
For a clear drink of kindness

You are my last frontier
The wild place I dare not enter
Lest I be reduced to the lost child

Turn around and look
Into the confusion
You have left in your wake

Do you have the courage
To step in front of the mirror
That hides nothing

See into yourself
Into the tangle of torment
That cries for your attention

I will meet you on that shore
Perhaps not in this life
Naked in our willingness

To enter the maelstrom
Where we may be released

NEARLY

For my father

I

Face the turbulence, I look to the sea, hat lifting off and away
In the wind, the formless blows and throws me back
A sliver of seed finds its way through closed doors
I remember how this landscape cleansed and held you
        thin ribbon of sanity renewed
        by union with water, salt and sun.
Today I understand, lost man, how endless days
        on these western shores might have
        transported you to Coney Island beaches
        and a King's Highway to another promise.

II

Shoes, black and shiny with square toes,
        feet too large for the body,
Short, wiry, bow-legged, heels dug into the pavement
        Thrust you forward, shout: *out of my way.*
Bent forward, war-bruised, barrel chest and muscled
        The past of a Brooklyn tough
Long Roman face, square jaw, thin lips, almost aristocratic
        but for a large nose and small, almond-shaped eyes.
Your tall forehead slopes back from sculpted eyebrows,
        where large veins ripple under dark olive skin.
In anger, they pop and the nostrils, like a stallion, flair
Your loud voice radiates
        vehement waves that part the familial sea,
        a raging Moses carrying tablets of loss.
Yet, there is a delicacy beneath rough gestures
        perceptible when you think no one is watching,
        lit cigarette, curling smoke
        and a far-off look in your eyes

III

It was 1930, you were selected to be the one to drop out,
a boy who couldn't sit still at school, eager to work
for a butcher by day, in hopes your father might notice
when he found the food you put on the table
Later, a handball champ, handsome with a wide smile
fragile heart, street smart, quick tempered you'd
give your shirt to whomever confessed the need
A second world war took you into the Pacific and injury
brought you home again to meet the glowing Rose
at Far Rockaway and marry her a bare 6 months later
black tux and white satin. Just kids.
When it all began to dissolve and turn sour

Cold winters and your son's rheumatic fever drove you west
chasing health, hope, a better life, like your Sicilian
matri e patri
who landed on this continent barely fifty years before
Your daughter, born in 1951, remembers many moves before
the family landed at last, in the big white house
with low rent, nearly donated by the wily Minnie
Cordeiro,
Portuguese immigrant and matriarch,
disappointed by both
her own husband and son, whose favor you won
Finally, a sense of home, rooms to retreat to, doors to close,
the place where future memories could congeal.
Hub of holiday dinners where your brothers and their families
gathered, your table's abundance overflowing
then trailing off unmet
resentment filling your plate, pride distilled to bitters.
By then you were held in the arms of a mistress,
once family friend.
Turning from you, your Rose befriended her young daughter
filled her ears with the family secrets
The girl's heart dilated between love and hatred, as she
attempted to hold these stories in a neutral chamber of her
heart:

IV

Wild boy, you hid the family cat under the lid of a grand piano, ran off
in fits of laughter, fully enjoying your show of mischief
Then a gang of boys, a rape, hushed whispers and the birth of shame
In 1929, you watch your father, crushed by the Great Depression,
lose his hard-earned immigrant wealth, his pride, himself.
Twenty years later, you bring *matri e patri* home to your young family,
Conversing in the language of the old country

V

Desire, your birthright, repressed, oppressed, lewdly locked
drags its heavy tail, creeps from the
shadows, hunts and devours you while I hold my breath, am watchful
of your next move, tracking when you will rise after laying
in bed for days at a time, small blue pills your only companion.
I tiptoe past your room, the door cracked, hear your
heavily-drugged breath, smell the struggle and dread
the possibility of disturbing the nightmare, the beast
within the man I sometimes recognize as father

VI

On your better days, you laugh loudly, contagiously, you call me
"moon child" denying any responsibility
for my origins, in spite of our resemblance
I am glad when you sell the house, move south and west
to the sea, salty waves nearly washing you clean, hot sun
burning the layers into air-born ash
lift up and away in the marine breeze
Still, you were eager to die

leaving us without instructions on where to dig for cash-filled jars.

VII

You prayed for days like this:
A pure white seagull skims the undulating surface
the tips of his wings barely touching down,
sea water fans, a flash of rainbow crescent
one wave builds, then breaks at my feet.

ROSE

i've got two feet in one shoe
your way of complaining
we would laugh and nod
i wanted to suggest freeing
a foot or finding the other shoe
to stride through life balanced
arms outstretched & free
laugh and the world laughs
with you... the other thing
you would say mostly to me
...cry and you cry alone
there was no kleenex in the house
only toilet paper and never enough

some crack under pressure
highly organized carbon
with time and tension
becomes a diamond
you didn't wear your stone
nor did I when you died,
but i kept your old slippers
both of them by the nightstand
for two years
the sound of your voice
on the rotary phone still
crackled in my ears
durable you rose
where you couldn't grow
again and again and stayed
diamond dust

NOTHING BUT

for my niece Michelle Carbonaro

A moment in time captured
and magnetized on the fridge
your smiling face
your little boy laughing
your girl's one curious eye
my closest living relative
what have I missed?

Shutter clicks, aperture open
the void has been chasing me
all night, siren wails in my belly
gnaws at the gash of sadness
almost like a daughter
which makes me not a mother
mine told me too much
I could tell you the whole story
open like the sky and pour
the whole truth down
but another fire calls your name
in the night & my
fuzzy-headed prayer
floats up to follow

There is time enough
a chancc to conncct thc dots
faces, hands & hearts
still dangle in your field
while mine are moving
surely and quietly away
like the rapidly expanding
universe

IL FRATELLO, LA SORELLA / THE BROTHER, THE SISTER

Again the words slip through
my effort to sleep
May your soul be at peace
May your spirit be released
a sweet mantra sings
since your death
Deep silence surrounds me
wholly unexpected
bewildering, yet
I turn toward the grief, a slow-
moving freight train

You, who tore a path through life
dark angel, hauled ass
on your Harleys
Reckoned the spectrum from
fucking, scrapping & swinging
to buying, selling & building
A fortress where *le bellezze dai*
capelli scuri della famiglia –
the dark-haired beauties
Of your family fell through the cracks,
one forever, one for just a while

This *bellezza dai capelli scuri,* waiting
on the sidelines, neatly placed
to mop up the blood, pleased
to celebrate births, prepped
to sing at weddings, poised
to bury the dead, finally
L'ultimo in piedi, last one standing
lights a candle to the force you
were, its long flame burns
without a flicker . . . for me,
Tutto e nuove, everything is new

BUTTERFLY BANDAGE

With the fecundity of rabbits they come
words like trails of ants in search of sugar
syllabic pheromones attracting their kin
like bees fiercely flapping wings over honey
faithful hive mates laboring as one
these words seek me out!
Super glue for a heart cleaved
A translation for ventricles that lack
the clotting agent of shared vocabulary
stems the bleeding
as medicine swirls
a scattered mind
bends the arc
of primal flight
to murmuration
to common song
Can you save us: stanza
sonnet, ode, lift us like prayer
gift us the keen eyes of a hawk?
break greed's curse, so kinship
may include all sentient beings
I bow to the poem's will
to turn the tide
as a compass guide
stay for the runaway train
stent for the closed vein
A butterfly bandage
hold what can hold
all still together
a healing from
the inside out

LISTEN

"What is to give light must endure burning" - Victor Frankl

fires of grief
burn thru every pore
every crevice of self
every belief held tightly
even of inherent goodness

beliefs fail us now
watch as they dissolve
fly away on the breeze
ashes in free flight
no time to bid farewell

fully awake, eyes wide
turning toward the east
the return of light, a new day,
surrender to who knows what
gently hold the darkness

as revealed in outer form
step forward in terror
and in trust, asking:
how can i be of use
this burning one?

carry the torch
of initiated innocence
stumbling at times
falling, yet knowing
the fire will light a way

beyond a shallow safety
to a new land where
the heart of the world
pulses and sings

somewhere between
terror and trust runs
the deeper river
of resolve, and there
we will reside, there

the sun outshines
the fires of grief
a prayer rises up
in a yet unspoken
language of light

BLACK & WHITE

Clutching a white cloth in her hand
she could no longer carry the weight
of much more than one lifetime
in her diminutive black body.
She struggled to stay erect upon
the hard wooden chair, next to her son.
Her face was wet with weeping

His cocky lawyer with a slick defense
could not save him from consequence
the voices when they finally won
thrusting him toward
his own enactment of justice
How could this be her son?
His face now glazed and numbed

She held it all for him
and felt she might explode
into so many pieces of a life undone
She thought of the other mothers,
The ones she had seen on TV
How they managed to appear strong
Beneath the weight of Victim v. Perp

She looked at the young woman
and the young woman looked back
Wet eyes and all lines blurred
Justice dropped her blindfold
Pierced both hearts
As the courtroom dropped away
Scales hung in perfect balance.

HASHTAG

remembers how it started
recalls how far it went

mistook fear for fascination
overtaken by the scent
of his own pounding flesh
so caught in the obsession
so sure she wants to know
once more shaken by the sight
of a girl, of a woman

sought domination, even then
saying "it will be our secret"
sensing rising trepidation
but she wants a door held open
so she'll comply
she'll be complicit
perhaps lose track of who
did what
and when

#hetoo
will count on her confusion
will twist the facts to suit his sin

as she begins to lose her compass
in the vortex of his spin

BLUE MEANIES

I

Age 9, curiosity exposed, it
almost crushed her, the big wheel
she was fast, always got away
born in the year of the rabbit
ran like the wind for cover
kept her eyes peeled
ears up for a pin drop
hop hop hop

you wanna ride this chopper?
eyes grown wide, she trusted
no helmet, hard seat, *hold on*
sister! gripped his wide ribs
held her breath on hard turns
tears ran down his face
was it wind or for his sins?

May 12, 1972, Union Square
a stick slipped through spokes
brought that motor cop down
someone lit a quick match &
the flames went up, oh shit
chaos erupted, then came
Reagan's men in riot gear
hop hop hop

heads cracked, blood spilled
pure rage &
just another genocide
big wheel keeps on turning
she didn't always get away

II
Stop running rabbit, notice
the big wheels everywhere
their tracks leave ruts
in the earth, in our lives
drive a stick in the spokes
but don't get caught
the man cherishes his wheels
his starched blue uniforms

women prefer hoops
don't jump through them
stay vigilant & seek out
your kin, form a rabbit
brigade, practice kindness
and remember how
to make good trouble

III
The boy on the chopper
has come to a halt, it's 2024
the rabbit rests. past battles,
accompanying cacophony
fade into the blue

FALLING

this morning i hiss at life
at the aching in my body
faux stabs at patience
toss me thru the long night
of restless dreams and now
awake i study the sounds
of your deep sleep

the coffee is bad here and costs
a pretty penny (like everything else)
perhaps i am a spoiled tourist
in the land of *uno mas*
looking but missing the tired
dark eyes of a hungry child
who pays daily for my ease
and entertainment

how has it come to this
decades of dredging the
depths of salient passages
from dog-eared books
highlighted, underlined
nearly memorized teachers
arriving at this morning
your spacious smile

i cringe at the brightness
turn away from food while
you gently draw the curtains
stay close & soft beside me
while i spin inward
skyward spread-eagled
i stare at the ceiling
and fall upward

YOU TURN

In the absence of kindness
take one deep breath
and then let it go
into the heat of confusion
or an echoless emptiness
where it may be swallowed up
like a dove in a black hole
listen to it coo gently in the dark

The next breath may disorient you
that's a good sign
go ahead
lose your way
your point
your imitation
of someone you don't
now recognize

You've made a U-turn
and like a boomerang
struck by lightning
random acts of kindness
now seem as natural
as being breathed into self
one who has forgiven
any part of the whole that
might have believed
you were not enough

ELEVENTH HOUR

i will
start over
one giant step
back to square one
the first hop-scotch box
there, balance precariously
on one foot….barely breathing
only this time shyly smiling instead
of biting my lip and twitching my face
it doesn't matter now if I lose my balance
and fall completely outside the box and never
again follow the rules of a game created by men
strutting on the cutting edge of lust and destruction
today trading in reason for the willingness to surrender
the sequential and linear for the outbreath of thirty-three
whirling dervishes at the center of this soul's insistent longings
finally knowing I might enter any square at any time (or not)
now finding myself (and you) at the portal of this eleventh
hour, entering into a room without walls, floor or ceiling
silent and still in a rapidly expanding limitless space of
requiescence, no direction, no pushing or pulling of
any kind, only forgiveness and an abiding trust in
the unfolding of each moment bubbling into
the next and the next one bursting with a
light of its own which is something like
love and is accompanied by a hum
so deep it readily travels thru all
matter, it carries us into, over
silt, a river's forgotten flow
eddys release: old selves
float, then ripple out
beyond any need
to be defined
by what
was

HARBINGER

A cloak-of-mourning came to me today
ivory and indigo-adorned wings brush
        the air like lace, her burgundy-
        black beauty softens secrets
Cracks open what soul hid from psyche

From a cornice of winter cold
She arrived . . . harbinger of a new spring
Innocence unlocked
        somewhere between memory and déjà vu
        a young girl with open arms
        chases butterflies. She too emerging!
I am returned
To the trail, where I can find no sign
of the darkly graced wings in any direction.
Had I missed it?

I feared I had lost her in the gulf
Between a child's joy and a woman's sorrow
But she lands. At my feet.
        Flitting down the path to safety
My hand lifts to the sky
Waiting.   Breathless.   Out of time.

Wings fluttered
She is swirling, spiraling
Upward in wide circles
Dancing into an open sky

EMPTY POCKETS

holding out for what I sense
will never be
won't bring it
while that from which
the daily news is made
still tries to spin it

can voting for
the lesser of two evils
pin it, while those
who build the bombs
who fund the slaughter
of so-called "lesser breeds"
(they that follow foreign creeds)
are sure *their* might
will win it

one side hope
the other fear
the coins that buy
you nothing dear

*   *

hope
the acorn
who knows she's an oak
out of the way
of hording squirrel or hungry jay
embryonic roots push down
her cotyledons swell & crown
the shell cracks wide
whatever blocks is pushed aside
reach up & cry become
one with endless sky

PLATINUM 2021

I can go years without breaking anything
Yesterday, a new white bowl slipped from my hand
This Christmas Day there were no illusions

Today, Kwanza begins and my purple neti pot
followed it, that perfect sphere of containment
Am I practicing letting things slip away?

I have a replacement
Alan bought it for me years ago
seeing how attached I was to the ritual

As I care for him
his care for me translates itself
into a continuity that will linger long after

This year brought much we could have
done without. Surge after surge of a virus
in all its variations, dangerous attempts at normality

Treason shook the shaky ground we thought
we held… the ice melts, wind whips
death cones, while those who can slow

This train down, don't do enough. Where is the deep
breath without the wail? There is no respite here
I am not ready to say goodbye

Even as I acknowledge the inevitable. The many losses
that we carry in our hearts
carve a space for what's to come, known, unknown

Small acts. That's it.
Not the golden rule but the twist
Treat others as *they* wish

NINE YEARS, A GHAZAL

Your curiosity caught up with mine, now beginning to begin
Aries' passion flaming higher as we plow, beginning to begin

Music of the diasporas, you on the airwaves, the breath of life
Currents in the Mad River, we in the Tao, beginning to begin

Old wounds held with soft touch & sight, scars wane with song
& poetry's light
Your fears point where I can't see, you on the prow,
beginning to begin

You turn away when the conman wins, I descend and in
darkness spin
You nudge me toward completion, triumph somehow,
beginning to begin

How can this be, we toast release, as fires burn our community
Your grief & too much weight on a tender bough,
beginning to begin

I take flight, hitting a wall, your waters damned, our plans
stuck in a stall
Alzheimer's dumped in our trembling hands, our vow,
beginning to begin

Six months after Alz drops in to squat, cancer mets come to tie
the knot
I ask to marry whom death has chosen: thou,
beginning to begin

Tens of thousands dead from a plague; your mind falls away,
entreaties vague
Time to cohabitate with your cat: meow, beginning to begin

Beginning of the end, all work stopped, except to touch, to
  bear, to tend
To let you go where the dead must go & ciao,
  beginning to begin

A SHAKESPEAREAN APOLOGY

My fear, again, has birthed an ugly child
While you retreat to nurse a bitter gut
And I, adrift on waves that toss me wild
Pray that our precious love I have not cut
How may I calm this frightened fiend within
That takes me by surprise and steals my tongue
My goodness yanked below the roots of sin
Where songs of deepest trust remain unsung
Such presence true, love's gift I've rarely known
Yet quick am I to question and to doubt
May courage risk my heart to all we've sown
And grow our cleansing sage, even in drought

It is forgiveness that I ask for here
Committing kindness to replace the fear

PSYCHE'S OTHER BOX

This one's yours to behold / to
reclaim / to revisit / however

Do not organize / alphabetize /
digitize & by no means analyze

Realize its beauty at a glance
keep it close / the sacred file

Holy coffin of remembrance /
colorful / haphazard / like the

Life you've known / reaching
for the loose notes / tucking

Them back in / faux neat / until
such time arrives to unlock / to

Tip the vault / memories now
but a flurry of butterfly wings

All to be read by those who
thought they knew you / by

Those who knew they loved
you / your ribboned & rough

Edges

INCANDESCENCE

Were you teasing me?
I kneeled at your feet
head on your belly
hands on your heart
Are you praying, you asked
Am I god, you asked

Not getting it
I shook my head
and drew away
Mute
Sadness dug a trench in my chest
and planted a prayer:

May our love be an open highway
nothing to pass by
and no one is left behind
no end in sight
just wide expanse
moving in both directions

May our love be large enough
for restless ruminations
high beams for when the light dims

May our love be a refuge
with wide safe shoulders
to pull over and rest

For a while
My head on your belly
My hands on your heart

LEAN MEAT

Listen, my friend
He does not bring me down
I bring me down
the girl held hostage inside
the lucky lie that life
cleaves clean and easy

I watch as he holds what is left
in balance with what gets cut away
how my own struggles are now
impossible for him to hold
yet, he lays beautiful hands
on my skin as a ripe plum

He once delivered fresh, organic food
to our kitchen, cooking with focus and care
Loyal and committed, at times with an edge
like a knife that pares the fat
to leave the lean meat of truth
to chew, to swallow, to digest

In the midst of this gnawing grief
When so many others hunger
I cannot moan for more
To fill me. The taste of promises
Forgotten and forgiven.

OUR LAST SPRING

the veil is thin today
branches reach out
caressing this grief
bursting their buds
even as he is dying
exploding with life
even as death nears
blossoms with tongues
it's going to be fine, he
says "you will go (on)"
this is birth in reverse
a soul will be released
suspended on a fresh
breeze, given back

plants speak, birds
will call, earth will
spin & sky will open
into a great pause, a
stillness within shift
everything is going
to be okay, exhale
he may have one day
or many days, no matter
wander between what
used to be necessities
no need to outshine
yourself, trust the cycle
first disintegration, the

long dark & waking
you will churn on
the threshing floor
of loss, new seeds
will ricochet, burrow
sprout, push up and

out from the deep
teeming muck, yes
there's no denying
what is coming
or so much life
climbing like a
hungry vine out
of a longing for
what we grew

FLOATING

pressed to the edge of our circumference
the fraying threads of once-assumed normality
barely held, loose ends, circumvented lines
of thought, lost then found, then lost again

you won't remember where I was today
or who I went with or why, you
wander outside your old lines
perhaps now finally free
of hope, of hoping that this might go away
dissolve like a bad dream

free to let words dance in strange configurations
of delight and defiance, language stinging and
soothing your stunned queen bee
worried
you will lose your way back
home
still,
I celebrate how your fingertips know how to find me
your lips meet mine, we move and breathe together
reaching for that embrace beyond knowing
the taste of tears

I will still be here when I am not
a lock I can't pry open
Today is going to be a good day!
a current I tread madly

somehow my body remembers dead-man's float
I lay back and bare my face
towards your words

REVOLVING

Wind picks up palm fronds
blows them back like the hair
on a screaming rock star
Let's get outta here, he wails
  the plane is on the runway

Urgency chases me up the stairs
suitcases lie open everywhere
Immobilized by impossible choices
I head for the shore, one last glimpse
  before abandoning paradise

I want off this shrinking island
Lifetimes of oceans closing in
but I keep missing the flight
there's always too much
  to pack, too little time

Perhaps I misjudged this all along
Distracted by my own story
I got your call through the astral plane
Time to fly away on those big wings
  back at last to the mainland

Now, I'm nobody here
highways stretch for miles
cars rush who knows where
I'll give up this tight journey
  spread out in all directions

COURAGE

Your battle had been chosen
in the war that never ends
before your number was called

Standing on the empty rooftop
USC's view of a raging fire below
afforded you a new perspective

Roaming the streets of Watts
after the smoke cleared
you were called there to serve

To fight an intractable & vile
enemy known as white supremacy
young black men, your teachers

The diploma your parents coveted
never materialized, however
your PhD in *eyes wide open*

Continued to your death
Seeing injustice as you did
set your course as a man

In a world you hoped to change
it started by saying NO to the draft
and YES to remaining in the country

OK to a month in jail and THANKS
to the judge who acquitted you.
I like to imagine what you said

In court when you stood up
and said NO to war, YES to
teaching, to a stint in seminary

To fatherhood, activism, the healing arts.
The Vietnam war didn't need you
You were called by other brothers.

CRASH COURSE

Not only my plate   the table overflowed
Overwhelm the rule   not the exception   clutter
Our house your mind eventually my mind   Folks
brought food too much food the table overflowed
Not just food schedules, meds, cards, flowers   Care
calendars yours mostly mine when possible   Holding
the pen as tightly as my gut, my jaw, held me   Placing
one foot, one plan, in front of the other   I forgot how
to swallow in the midst of your care   Was diagnosed
with a stricture in my esophagus   A knot of NO
There was so much to keep track of
There was so much pain to hold to feel to release
There was so little time

Earning a PhD in caregiving was not what I wanted to say
YES to when I said YES to you, to us, to our future   But love
the love rolled right over my fear of watching you slip away
while fulfilling the assignment as your sole caregiver   YES:
all I could say was YES   YES to every NO you shouted at me
YES to watching you lose track of your life while I tracked
you   YES to your denial of Alzheimer's   YES to stage 4
cancer (the saddest gift that took you before you forgot us all)
YES to using myself up   to the dearth of empathy, gratitude &
help from those who expected nothing less   YES to my
ensuing resentment YES to your improvised songs, gibberish &
my desire to join in on the silliness   YES to your wild
laughter! I bow to YES & its ability to annihilate any
resistance to all that was beyond my control

YES to the blood, incontinence, to your questions about the
blood YES to No More Food   to liquid methadone   to
morphine & anti-psychotic meds   to the mind-numbing cream
when you wouldn't open your mouth   YES to the last time we
touched foreheads   YES to your last breaths   your orgasmic,
birth-like death   to the smile that your skeletal face assumed
two hours after   YES to leaving my body for months and just

finding it again   YES to finally slowing down   to stopping   to
my own deep breaths   to seeing you everywhere   even as I
continue to grieve your loss in new & unexpected ways YES
to a blood moon 49 days after your death   YES to not
knowing why

BEAR

Love is more powerful than death -- Neem Karoli Baba

In the crumbling barn of my mind
chaos chases me from room to room
My beloved dies before my eyes
I cannot save him. I am suffocating

This place is burning and I have to get out
Now. Pushing out on the heavy double door
I leap into the fresh air and land hard
on the ground below, you just behind

Were you there with me all this time?
Adrenaline propels my legs forward
as I feel your massive heat in the air
your heaving breath on my back

If I can just leap this next barrier: I fly
up (and what I hope) is over. Damn
I'm caught on the ledge. Take me now Bear
Your authority comes from the Great Spirit

Is this the end? Yes, the end of running
of struggling. Receiving the gift of your weight
this somebody softly dissolves into the
ferocity of love   I can do this

LOST, NOT LOST

wandering familiar streets, lost
earbuds stuffed under a tight cap
an old friend on the other end
doing a thing he was never
very good at, listening

my man just went into hospice
I explained and who knows
how long… my friend's voice
was like a light pulsing
through underground cables

his wife wants to join in
she's still a stranger really
but knows what those with
alzheimer's need, how to talk,
when to bring out the stuffed toy

how to stay bright, cheery, how
not to correct, react or even
make the wrong face, how to
set yourself on the shelf of
service. the tyranny of positivity!

suddenly i recognize the street
I'm on, a block from home
it's sunny now and warm, my
agency rising like a raven from
a redwood branch, ready

to meet my mate in joyous flight
tumbling into the giddy play
of our days now, beyond language,
intentions, plans, far beyond
even the best advice

ON THE NECESSITY OF THE FELINE

I am introduced
though you may just hear meow
listen more closely
like you, I am expressive
fluent in myriad ways

The year I moved in
was a challenge for us all
sick man, woman, cat
doing my best to slow you
so my man could rest

A leash, for a cat?
Who created such a thing
with a halter, too?
I *can* run when a car comes
Too much love: suffocating!

We prefer to live outside
with ladybugs, birds
the occasional canine
is greeted by hiss & claw
and is not welcome!

I warm to woman
slowly she recognizes
I am number one
to her beloved husband
it is I he pets each night

Roaming in the dark
do not fear, I will return
enlivened & calm
I won't jump on your counters
I will eat what you feed me

And still leap at mice
devour them in your sight
prove my loyalty
my devotion beyond doubt
please clean my cat box

I feel his illness
I will not leave his side now
more like dog than cat
as he wanders, we are there
we will see him through

Gazanias hide me
from unwelcome guests & dogs
from one we can't hide
death will come and take our man
the light will go out

Like him, I lose weight
with no desire for life
we sleep day & night
many think I may die, too
they don't understand my role

Call me guardian
find rest & refuge with me
I am his shadow
even as his spirit leaves
I do not leave the deathbed

My paw on your hand
we move slowly through winter
I sleep near your head
so you are now my person
I walk across your pillow

Another winter
I may join our lost man then
into the glitter
beyond a blue sky, with a
deep bow from your grateful cat

Don’t try this alone
at home, solo, with few friends
loss requires touch
a loyal cat on your lap
where your beloved still purrs

AFTER WE READ DIPRIMA

They both thought it was over:
finding one to call companion, let
alone soul mate, let alone beloved
He thought that corner of his heart
dried and ready for the weed pile
For her, trust was trapped in a rusty fist

Now she flies back to the mornings
he waited long before she arose, his
engine humming in anticipation
for a tousled, smiling woman
to unlock the door, make strong
coffee, kiss his day awake

But his shadow moves across
ice on the wings of lonely nights
she lights an American Spirit
sips Irish whiskey, listens
to the music of bird call and traffic
threading their downtown lingo as she
blows embers onto a stick of sage

You are powerful, he told her
again and again, until she believed

You were the one
she whispers back

DEEP SONG

Memories swirl me in circles
a dizzying roulette wheel of
loss and lasting riches: wheels
coming to rest on Haight St.
a colorful sidewalk before us
we step out, we hold hands, we
wander with tourists, with locals
the homeless, the glazed over
looking for their next hit

You know fashion. You check
labels. You spot the elegant
the funky, the uniquely me
a few righteously, perfectly you
threads for yourself, for your kids
your grandkids, not just clothes
woven bags for holding the finds
of a lifetime, bundled, lastly saved
with purpose and stones, twigs, awe

We catch the bus back, the bus you
warned me about at the beginning
of our trip "it might get crazy" you
laugh; lots of folks on board: family,
extended family, old lovers, friends,
students, breath of life beings,
laughter and love floating, as
hot dogs & joy are served upfront
duende silently riding in the back

Smooth times
rough times
uncut
genuine
precious
like each grain of a sand mandala

flying off the wheel of a self
released, to be
remembered

RED. SUDDEN RED.

After Robert Hass

The dream, a sacred landscape
wedding the possible to a hidden
portal, one the dreamer might not
reach any other way, in the wee hours
the revelation color of blood, cut by
a softer blade of renewal

In droves we come, all unbidden
guests to my elementary school
to this room with wood floors
and a black grand piano but
no pianist, center stage, open
and ready to be played for
some astonished gathering

Bride and groom walk together
from one corner of the large space
to the next, each of four directions
an altar, to meet lost layers of the
masculine, the feminine, before
tying the proverbial knot, a slip
knot of fragile, intimate complexity

The groom, in black tux and dark
lustrous shoes, kneels at the feet
of his bride, silent in her long
white dress, she gently touches
the crown of his head, as he weeps
endless apologies, all crimes
of his kind repented

Lastly, we walk in a line to the open
piano past its empty bench and back
down the main aisle, each of us
returning a newly shrived self

sudden red circles the hall
flutters at my right shoulder

To the back of my head she flies
Dissolving delivering
her lust, her fire

THE DEVICE

I couldn't look at it anymore
It sat on your box of ashes
for almost 10 months. I think you
would approve since you no longer
need it: no body > no mouth
I confess to having no idea how
much to save of who you were

A half-mouth of false teeth, metal palate
gave you something of a down-and-out
appeal, not the straight white, perfect
teeth of your Palo Alto upbringing which
were eventually too much to maintain
along with troubled skin, family smiles
became a constant drain on the wallet

At a huge cost, I saved the one back
molar that held it in place. You thought I
was nuts but it was worth it: you could
chew your diminishing intake of food for
almost two more years. You could mug for
the camera. You could grin at me, you fool

As your filters fell away, the device would
come out to play: as a crazy moment's toy or
just to annoy. The places those teeth traveled
stirring memories forever implanted

TED

It takes years to figure out
that an old cat is a girl's best friend
He no longer wants to run off in the night,
on the prowl & now needs you
more than you need him
He waits patiently to be fed, washes, then
crawls into your bed each night,
his warm, satin fur next to your belly
He literally purrs you into a soft, smiling mass
& the deepest sleep you've ever known

Sometimes you wake aroused, wondering how
his magic goes there, too
Curiosity could walk you toward the computer,
googling your way into such feline secrets
Instead, you lie there, while he lays his face close
against yours & waits for your touch
It is nearly pitch black in the night but you know
he is watching you learn to purr

RETURN

If I could but fly away
Through a crack in the sky
I would take my leave

I would take my leave
On restless wings
Into the starry dark

Into the starry dark
Beyond the veil of sorrow
Into a blinding light

Into a blinding light
Our atoms would meet
In a glittering storm

In a glittering storm
Where nothing and no
One is left behind

And no one is left behind
And no one is left behind

OUT OF THE BLUE

For Tamsin Smith

she came down, an angel
at my beloved's request
I see you she said
I hear you I said
fly just high enough
she said so the wounds
of this world might singe
your heart but not your
wings. you can't save it all
(or yourself) from down here

utterances of a planet's unraveling,
its tender cries, its shouts of rage,
free jazz meets shakuhachi meets
tinnitus, the universal ring of deafening
silence, yet unheard above the pound
of war or annihilation of any resistance
in zones of interest, live to defy dystopia
& just keep breathing, oxygen on

remember your ancestors never
left you. so don't abandon them.
you were sent for a reason, no matter
the number of seasons it has taken
to arrive, fly no flag she says, sing no
anthem. trust in the bitch karma & its
mysterial ways. arrive naked at the polling
place, wearing only your dancing shoes.
we will meet you there, sans security
& ready to roll

Fran Carbonaro, 2017

Fran Carbonaro would say she was saved by the arts. She is the daughter of first-generation Sicilian-Americans whose roots were in Brooklyn before moving to the East Bay, where she was born in 1951. Her early years were a dance of straddling disparate realities and artistic devotion was the glue that held it all together. After moving to Sonoma County in 1976, Fran performed as a vocalist with rock bands, jazz ensembles and in local theater, which kept her on stage for many years. It was writing poetry that always brought her home. *Out of the Blue* is her first book.

Fran released *I'm Still Alive* in 2018, an album of spoken poetry and song. She. lives in Sebastopol, California, where she is a private vocal coach.

THE PAGE POETS SERIES

Number 1
Between First & Second Sleep by Tamsin Spencer Smith

Number 2
The Michaux Notebook by Micah Ballard

Number 3
Sketch of the Artist by Patrick James Dunagan

Number 4
Different Darknesses by Jason Morris

Number 5
Suspension of Mirrors by Mary Julia Klimenko

Number 6
The Rise & Fall of Johnny Volume by Garrett Caples

Number 7
Used with Permission by Charlie Pendergast

Number 8
Deconfliction by Katharine Harer

Number 9
Unlikely Saviors by Stan Stone

Number 10
Beauty Will Be Convulsive by Matt Gonzalez

Number 11
Displacement Geology by Tamsin Spencer Smith

Number 12
The Public Sound by Marina Lazzara

Number 13
Record of Records by Rod Roland

Number 14
Strangers We Have Known by John Briscoe

Number 15
Cutting Teeth by Jesse Holwitz

Number 16
Other Scavengers by Lauren Caldwell

Number 17
Cueonia by Jesse Holwitz

Number 18
In the Museum of Hunting and Nature by Cynthia Randolph

Number 19
A New Species of Color by Tamsin Spencer Smith

Number 20
Busy Secret by Micah Ballard

Number 21
Out of the Blue by Fran Carbonaro

Made in the USA
Coppell, TX
12 June 2026

80728533R00049